SAP BUSINESS OBJECTS INSTALLATION AND CONFIGURATION

Installation, Server configuration steps, and CMC configurations

Venkatesh Paritala

Table of Contents

How to use the book Actively

This book offers information and steps for the installation and configuration of SAP BI 4.2. Please use this book alongside the Business Intelligence Platform Installation Guide for Windows and the Business Intelligence Platform Administrator Guide documentation provided by SAP.

This book is intended for system administrators who need to install and configure the system following the base installation of SAP BI 4.2.

The Purpose of Each Chapter

SECTION 1: INSTALLATION

1. Prerequisites This chapter will outline the necessary steps before installing the server. It will cover the actions required for service and admin accounts, the drivers that need to be installed, and the databases that must be set up, including the Audit database and CMS database, before installing the BO Server. Additionally, it will address considerations at the operating system level prior to the installation of the BO Server.

2.Installation of SAP BI 4.2 Provides a step-by-step guide for installing the BO Server.

3.Post Installation Configuration settings Explains the settings related to Tomcat configuration and SIA configuration.

4

SECTION 2: CMC

4.Adding License keys Describes the process of adding a license key for the BO environment in CMC

5.CMC Configuration wizard Provides a step-by-step guide on how to use the System Configuration Wizard.

6.Setting up the BOE services ports Explains the default port numbers assigned during installation, as well as how to assign port numbers for additional servers.

7.Destination job server setting Explains the destination settings for File System, FTP Server, and Email related to the Adaptive Job Server.

8.Auditing Configuration Explains the auditing settings related to auditing database configuration and specifies the set Events section for the events that need to be audited.

9.CMC Configuration Explains about Application CMC level configuration settings.

10.Hot Backup Settings Explains the settings related to hot backups and their necessity.

11.User Attribute management settings Explains the User Attribute management settings in CMC.

SECTION 3: CONFIGURATIONS

12.Windows AD Configuration
Provides an explanation of Kerberos authentication, including details about Service Principal Names (SPN). It also outlines the necessary configurations on the CMC side and the steps required at the Tomcat level.

13.Single Sign on Configuration
Explains the Keytab file and outlines the necessary changes to the properties files related to BILaunchpad, Global, OpenDocument files and Server.xml files which are located in the Tomcat directory.

14.SSL Configuration It outlines the steps for utilizing a keystore to generate a Certificate Signing Request (CSR). It also explains how to obtain the CSR signed by a Certificate Authority (CA) and how to install the Root, Intermediate, and Domain certificates.

SECTION 4 SERVER CONFIGURATIONS

15.Session Time out This chapter outlines the files that require updates to the session timeout settings.

16.Tomcat users xml Configuration
This explains the actions we need to take in the tomcat-users.xml file.

SECTION 7 IMPLEMENATION PLAN
26.Implementation Plan

SECTION 1 INSTALLATION

Chapter 1 Prerequisites

1. Setup the operating system.
2. Requests to be raised for creation of service accounts and adm accounts for particular servers.
3. Install SQL server drivers 2016 and check for the connectivity with the Database server.
4. Raise requests to disable the AV and Firewall prior to the installation.
5. Turn off DEP

Data Execution Prevention (DEP) is a built-in technology in Windows that helps protect your computer from executable code running from unauthorised locations. It achieves this by designating certain areas of your PC's memory as data-only, preventing any executable code or applications from launching from those regions.

Below screenshot shows, before DEP turn-off:

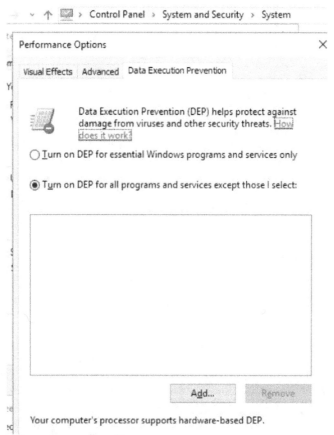

After DEP turn off:

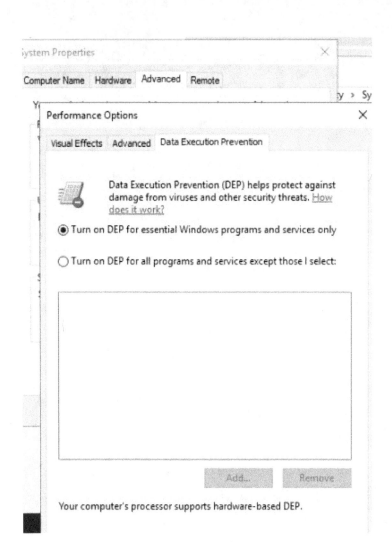

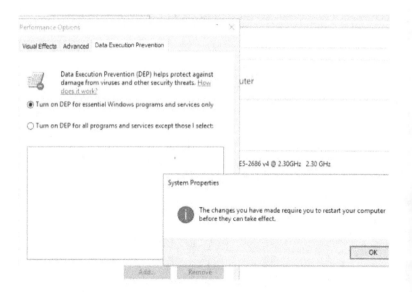

6. Change user Control Access to 'Never Notify'
User Account Control (UAC) is an essential
component of Windows security. It mitigates the risk
of malware by restricting the execution of malicious
code with administrator privileges.

Below is the screenshot taken before changing this option.

After changing this option to 'Never notify' it looks as below

7. Ensure that the service account you are using for the installation is part of the Administrators group.

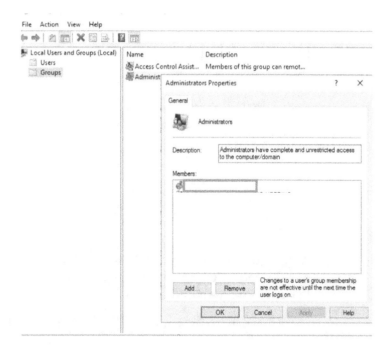

8. Enable 8-dot-3 support in Regedit.
Before Enable

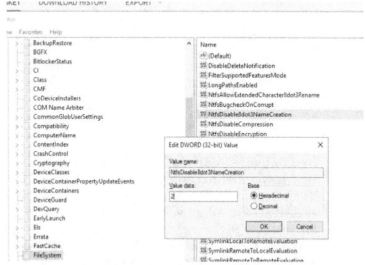

After enable I.e. changing this property value to 0 in regedit then click ok

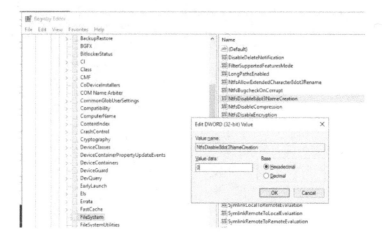

9. Assign the 'Service Account' user the "Act as part of the operating system" privilege in the Local Security Policy snap-in.

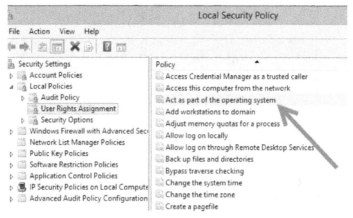

10. Configure Audit and repository Database
Decide whether to configure the SAP Business Objects BI Platform to use an existing installed database, such as SAP Sybase Adaptive Server Enterprise or Microsoft SQL Server via ODBC. Alternatively, you may choose to install SAP Sybase SQL Anywhere during the server installation at runtime.

11. Check for the Disk space and Memory prior to starting the installation.

12. Install supported Dot Net framework version 4.5.
13. Start the BO installation and do a prerequisite check.
14. The base install of SAP BI4.2 (I have considered to install this version as per my organization needs during the time of installation) should be completed on both Application & Web servers.

Please check the below:

http://<server name>:8080/BOE/CMC & http://<server name>:8080/BOE/BI should be working fine with Administrator credentials.

Terminology

Cluster: A cluster refers to two or more Central Management Servers (CMSs) that work together and share a single CMS database.

To consider a cluster in your environment Install a CMS and CMS database on machine A. Then Install a CMS on machine B.

By Point the CMS on machine B to the CMS database on machine A.

Chapter 2 Installation of SAP BI 4.2

Step1: Download the SAP BI 4.2 SP7 from SAP portal.

Step2: Copy the downloaded software file in installation BO server driver.

Step3: Extract the software folder on installation driver

Step4: Navigate to the path mentioned below, right-click on the setup.exe file, and select "Run as administrator."

Path:
E:\Software\SAP\51053643\DATA_UNITS\BusinessObjectsServer_win

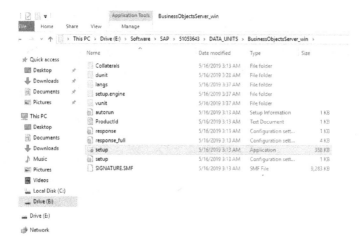

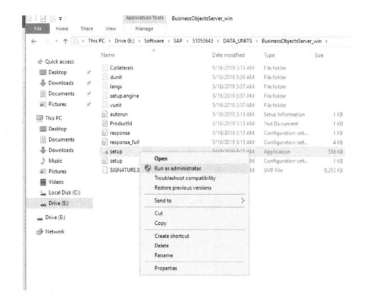

Step5: Select **English** as the language.

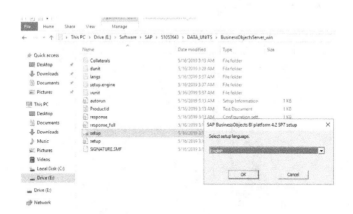

Step6: Ensure that all prerequisite checks are successful before clicking 'Next'.

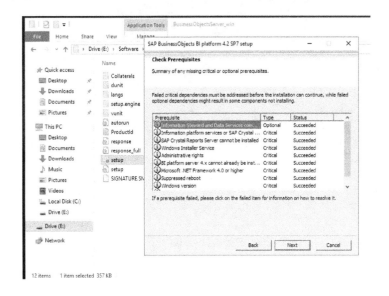

Step7: The installation welcome screen is displayed. Click 'Next' to proceed.

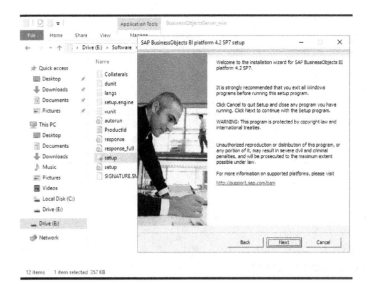

Step8: Accept the Licence agreement and click on next

Step9: Provide the Product key code

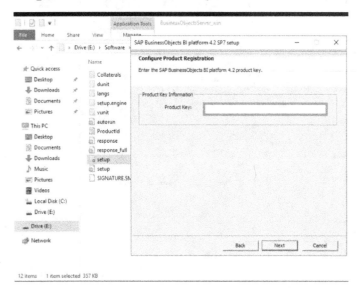

Step10: Select English from the language packs list and click on next

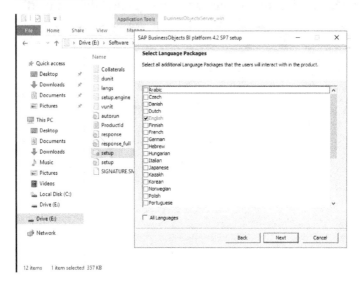

Step 11: Select Full build as the Install type and click next.

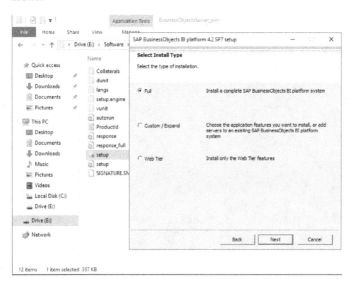

Step 12: Provide the destination folder path as E:\Program Files (x86)\SAP BusinessObjects\ and click on next

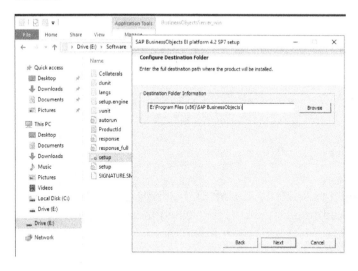

Step 13: Select Configure an existing database and click on next

Step 14: Select Microsoft SQL Server using ODBC from the CMS Database type selection and click on next

Step 15: Select Microsoft SQL Server using ODBC from the Auditing Database type selection and click on next

Step 16: Select the default Tomcat java web application server and automatically deploy web applications option from the Java web application server selection

Step 17: Select Configure and install subversion from version management selection and click on next.

Step 18: Provide the following SIA information and click on next

Node name: Please mention Required Name for Node
SIA Port: 6410

Step 19: Provide the following CMS port information and click on next

CMS Port: 6400

Step 20: Provide the following administrator Account and cluster key details:

Password: Please mention the password here

Cluster Key: Please provide the cluster key here

Step 21: Provide the system DSN information for CMS Repository

System DSN: BO_Repository

Database: BO_CMS_REPO_Test

Select use trusted authentication option

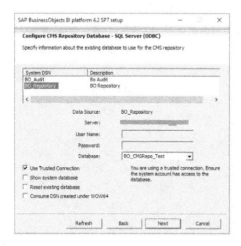

Step 22: Provide the system DSN information for Audit repository

System DSN: BO_Audit

Database: BO_CMS_Audit_Test

Select use trusted authentication option

Step 23: Provide the following information for Tomcat configuration and Use default settings and click on Next to continue

Connection port: 8080

Shutdown port: 8005

Redirect port: 8443

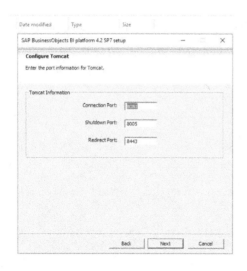

Step 24: Provide HTTP listening port as 6405

Step 25: Provide subversion repository information:

Repository name: LCM_repository

Repository port: 3690

27

Repository User Account: LCM

Repository Account password: Please enter the Password

Step 26: Select do not configure connectivity to SMD agent for solution manager agent

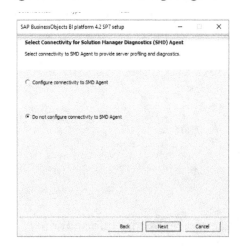

Step 27: Select do not configure connectivity to Introscope Enterprise manager

Step 28: Click on Next to start the Installation.

Step 29: Click on next to do Post installation steps and click on finish.

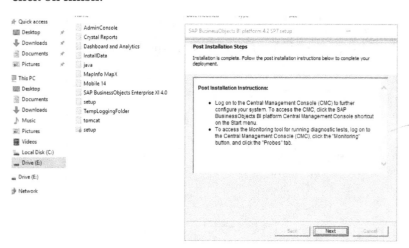

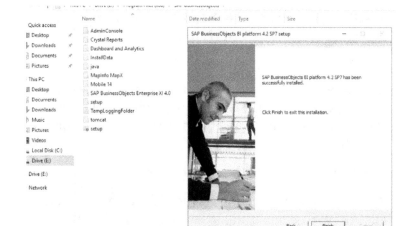

Chapter 3 Post Installation Configuration settings

In SAP BusinessObjects (SAP BO), Tomcat is the default web application server used for deploying applications such as BI Launchpad and Central Management Console (CMC).

SIA and Tomcat should run under service accounts.

Proper memory allocation is crucial for the performance of SAP BO web applications. By default, Tomcat has limited memory, which may need to be increased depending on the size and load of your deployment. When configuring Tomcat in the Server Intelligence Agent (SIA), several key settings must be considered to ensure optimal performance, security, and proper integration with the SAP BO platform.

3.1 Tomcat configuration

Step1: On BO server go to Tomcat configuration.

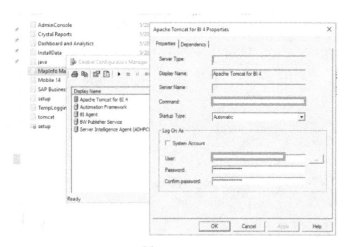

Step2: Select LOG ON tab.
Step3: Make Tomcat to run under service account (<Service Account>). Provide the service account details

Change memory settings as mentioned below.

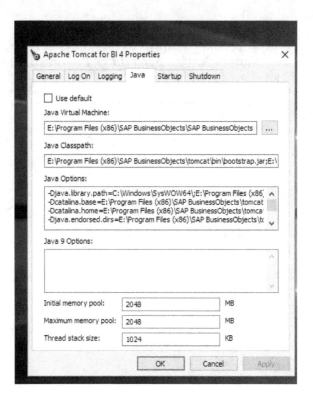

3.2 SIA configuration:

The Server Intelligence Agent (SIA) manages all BI platform servers and services. When you start the BI platform, the SIA starts automatically, along with any BI platform servers that are configured to start with it.

Step1: On BO server go to Central Configuration Manager.
Step2: Right click on the Server Intelligence Agent (SIA)
Step3: Select properties.

Step4: Make SIA to run under service account (service account your organization provided). Provide the service account details.

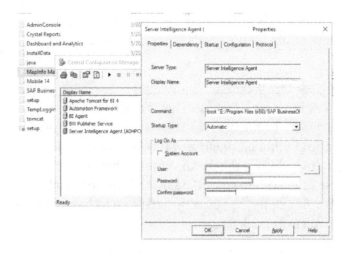

SECTION 2 CMC

Chapter 4 Adding License keys

SAP BusinessObjects products are licensed in various ways, depending on the needs of specific tools and services.

Named User Licenses: Each individual user who logs into the system requires a license. This is common for BusinessObjects tools such as Web Intelligence, Crystal Reports, and others. Concurrent User Licenses: These licenses are based on the maximum number of users who can access the system simultaneously. This approach allows for flexibility, as you only need to purchase enough licenses to cover peak usage.

Please add or update the license key in CMC > License Keys as shown below.

Central Management Console

License Keys

SAP BusinessObjects Business Intelligence Platform Premium Version

Currently deployed license keys (Select a key to see its licensing information.)

Add Key [   ] Add

[(Product code)   ] Delete

(Changes will take effect after you click "Add" or "Delete".)

SAP BusinessObjects Business Intelligence Platform Premium Version License Key Information

License Metrics	Selected Key	Total (All keys)	
Named Users:	-	0	
Concurrent Sessions:			Concurrent session based licenses (CSBL) can or
CPU Metric:	-	0	CPU license keys unlock unlimited access.
Expires:	Unlimited		

36

Chapter 5 CMC Configuration wizard

The System Configuration Wizard is a tool that you can use to configure your BI platform deployment. Simply and quickly, the wizard guides you through the basic configuration options, resulting in a working deployment using common settings such as these:

• Which servers you want to start automatically with the BI platform.

• Whether you want to optimise your deployment for maximum performance or for limited hardware resources.

• The locations of system folders.

By default, the wizard is set to run automatically when you log in to the Central Management Console (CMC), but you can change this setting within the wizard. Additionally, you can start the wizard at any time from the "Manage" area in the CMC.

After installing the BI4.2 platform, you will be prompted to use the System Configuration Wizard upon logging in as Administrator to the CMC.

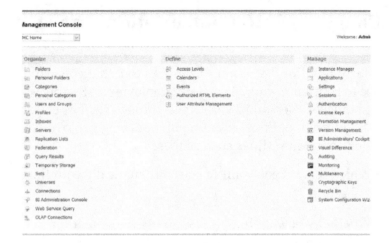

Login to CMC > Click on System configuration wizard

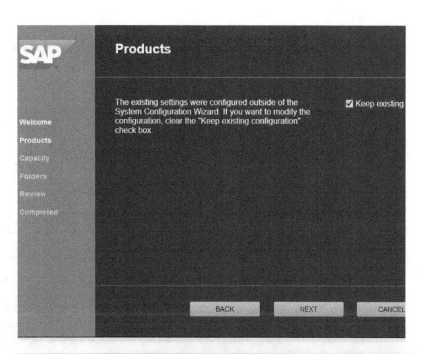

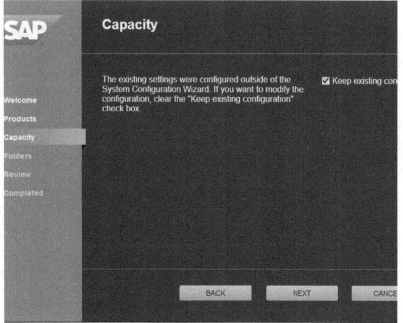

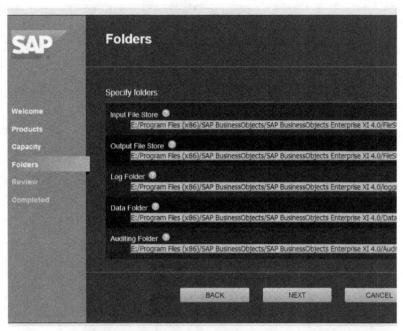

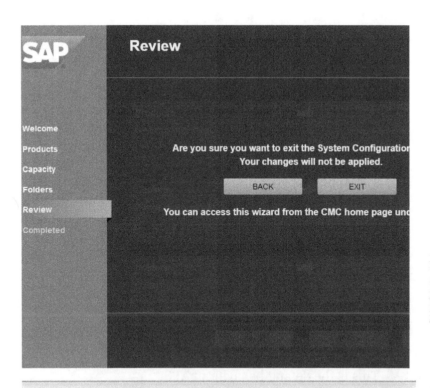

Review

Are you sure you want to exit the System Configuratior
Your changes will not be applied.

BACK   EXIT

You can access this wizard from the CMC home page unc

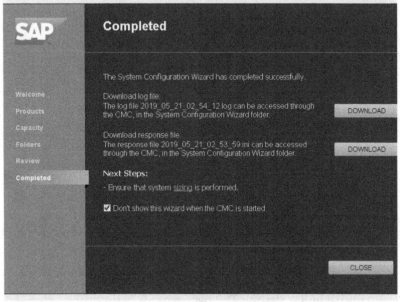

Completed

The System Configuration Wizard has completed successfully.

Download log file:
The log file 2019_05_21_02_54_12.log can be accessed through
the CMC, in the System Configuration Wizard folder.   DOWNLOAD

Download response file:
The response file 2019_05_21_02_53_59.ini can be accessed
through the CMC, in the System Configuration Wizard folder.   DOWNLOAD

Next Steps:

- Ensure that system sizing is performed.

☑ Don't show this wizard when the CMC is started

CLOSE

Chapter 6 Setting up the BOE services ports

The Adaptive Processing Server has approximately 23 common services. Running all services together simplifies deployment and reduces RAM requirements; however, it does not improve system scalability. To enhance system scalability, we split the APS into multiple Servers, which allows for better resource utilization and isolates specific tasks into Java containers. Each Java container has its own Java heap settings. While this approach increases RAM usage when the system is idle as well as when it is busy, it ultimately provides better system scalability.

The Adaptive Processing Server runs approximately 23 processes with a 1 gigabyte Java heap size.

This is the default behavior of APS.

RAM usage can increase when splitting the APS, but this approach offers improved system scalability.

Please keep in mind that when splitting the APS, it requires at least 16 GB or more of RAM per BI cluster.

Having 32 or 64 GB of RAM would be even more beneficial.

Some benefits include:

The BI Platform will have improved scalability and reliability. APS splitting is a good idea if you are reporting over BW.

System resources can be utilized more effectively, particularly RAM, for better system scalability.

Server-side process thread execution will be more efficient.

The system can support many concurrent users with less downtime.

1. DSL Bridge Services: Responsible for querying and serving data for reporting.

-DSL Bridge Service

-Web Intelligence (Interactive Analysis) Monitoring Service

-Security Token Service

-Tracelog Service (Included by default)

Recommended heap size: 4-8 GB

2. Search Service: Users can search for keywords in the BI Launchpad.

 - Platform Search Service

 - Tracelog Service (included by default)

Recommended heap size: 2-3 GB

3. OLAP Services: These enable the Web Intelligence analysis reporting tool and BEx web application service.

-Multi Dimensional Analysis Service

-BEx Web Applications Service

-Tracelog (Included by default)

Recommend heap size: 4-8

4. LCM Services: These handle promotion management and version control.

-Promotion (Life Cycle) Management Clear Cache Service

-Promotion (Life Cycle) Management Service

-Visual Difference Service

-Tracelog (Included by default)

Recommended heap size: 1-2 GB

5. Publishing Services: These handle the personalization of reporting publication.

- Publishing Post Processing Service

- Publishing Service

- Tracelog (included by default)

Recommended heap size: 2-4 GB

6. Web Intelligence Services

- Visualization Service

- Rebean Service

- Web Intelligence (Interactive Analysis) Monitoring Service

- Document Recovery Service

- Tracelog (included by default)

Recommended heap size: 2-4 GB

Steps:

Step 1. Login to CMC, Stop and disable APS

Step 2. Right click and uncheck automatically start server.

Host Identifiers:

- ⊙ Auto assign
- ○ Hostname [   ]
- ○ IP Address [   ] (IPv4) [   ] (IPv6)

☐ Automatically start this server when the Server Intelligence Agent starts

☐ Use Configuration Template

Services Manager

Step 3. Right-click on APS, select "Clone Server", rename it to "Adaptive Processing Services 1 (DSL Bridge)", and then click "Save and Close".

Step 4. Right-click on the newly cloned server and select "Select Services".

Step 5. Remove all services except for the DSL Bridge Service and Security Token Service.

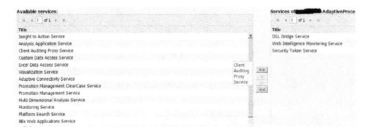

Step 6. Right-click and select "Properties." Go to the command line and change –xmx1g to –xmx4g. Then, check the option to automatically start servers.

The best way to do this is to select all, copy and paste it into Notepad for editing, and then copy and paste it back into the command line.

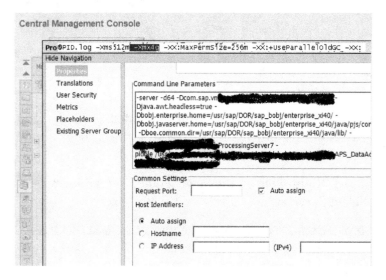

Step 7. Start and then enable the newly split server.

Please note that you should not start and enable the Adaptive Processing server, and it should not start automatically when the SIA restarts.

Step 8. Please follow the same steps to complete the rest, and configure all services to below port numbers:

The bold ones are already configured one when doing the deployment. Only configure the one in normal fonts.

Server name	Port
SIA	6410
Tomcat connection port	8080
Shutdown port	8005
Redirect port	8443
HTTP Listening port	6405
LCM Repository	6406
Adaptive Job server	6407
APS.Analysis	6408
APS.Analysis1	6440
APS.Auditing	6409
APS.Connectivity	6430
APS.Core	6411
APS.DF	6431
APS.Dataaccess	6412
APS.LCM	6413
APS.Monitoring	6434
APS.Search	6414
APS.Visualization	6435
APS.WEBI	6415
APS.WebIDSLBridge	6432
Central management server	6401
connection server	6416
connection server 32	6417

crystalreports2013processingserver	6418
crystalreports2013reportapplicationserver	6419
Crystalreportscacheserver	6420
Crystalreportprocessingserver	6421
Dashboardcacheserver	6422
Dashboardprocessingserver	6423
Eventserver	6424
Explorerexploartionserver	6425
Explorerindexingserver	6426
Explorermasterserver	6427
Explorersearchserver	6428
Inputfilerepositoryserver	6403
Lumira server	6437
Webapplicationcontainerserver	6412
Outputfilerepositoryserver	6404
Webinteliigenceprocessingserver1	6439
Webinteliigenceprocessingserver	6429

One of the examples with screen print can be found below:

Properties: **L.APS.Analysis**

Hide Navigation

Properties

User Security

Metrics

Placeholders

Existing Server Group

Command Line Parameters

-server -Dcom.sap.vm.tag=.   APS.Analysis -Djava.awt.headless=true
"-Dbobj.enterprise.home=E:/Program Files (x86)/SAP BusinessObjects/SAP
BusinessObjects Enterprise XI 4.0/" "-Dbobj.javaserver.home=E:/Program Files
(x86)/SAP BusinessObjects/SAP BusinessObjects Enterprise XI 4.0/java/pjs/container/"
"-Dboe.common.dir=E:/Program Files (x86)/SAP BusinessObjects/SAP BusinessObjects
Enterprise XI 4.0/java/lib/" "-Dboe.external.dir=E:/Program Files (x86)/SAP

-name .   ..   AdaptiveProcessingServer1 -pidfile "E:/Program Files (x86)/SAP
BusinessObjects/SAP BusinessObjects Enterprise XI 4.0/serverpids
/   ..   _   ..   .APS.Analysis.pid" -ns
..   :6400

Common Settings

Request Port: 6403   ☐ Auto assign

Host Identifiers:

◉ Auto assign
○ Hostname
○ IP Address   (IPv4)   (IPv6)

☑ Automatically start this server when the Server Intelligence Agent starts

Chapter 7 Destination job server setting

Login to CMC and right click on Adaptive job server > go to Destinations and set the destinations following below screen prints:

First add all destinations:

BI Inbox, File system, FTP server & Email

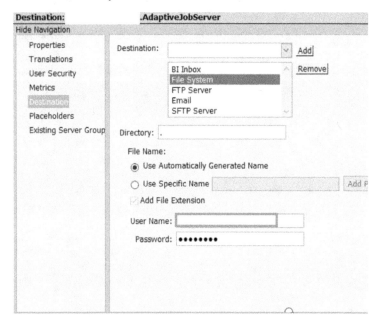

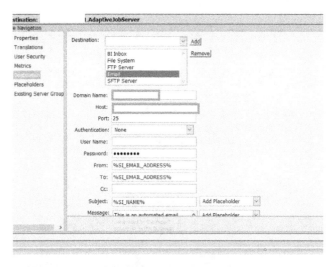

Configure email with below settings:

Host: Please provide host name as per your organization

Port: 25

From: %SI_EMAIL_ADDRESS%

To: %SI_EMAIL_ADDRESS%

Subject: %SI_NAME%

Message: This is an automated email generated by the report scheduler in the (<Organization Name>).

The scheduled report %SI_NAME% was successfully run starting at %SI_STARTTIME% and sent to you.

A link to your report is available here:

%SI_VIEWER_URL%

Check deliver document as attachment

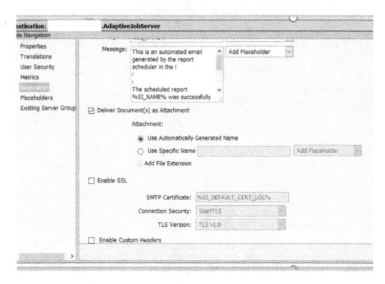

Configure File system with service account credentials as below:

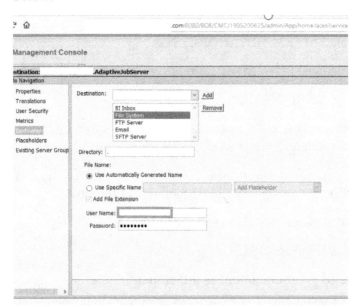

Restart SIA once you done with all configurations:

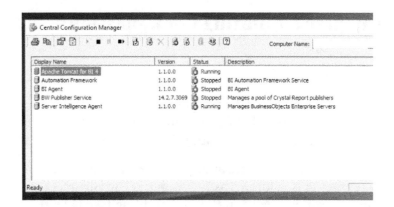

Chapter 8 Auditing Configuration:

CMS:

Only one CMS will write audit events to the Audit database. This is called the Auditor – the current auditor can be seen in CMC -> Auditing

Only one CMS will write audit events to the Audit database. This is known as the Auditor. The current Auditor can be viewed in CMC -> Auditing (see below).

A BO server that is generating the events is an Auditee, while all other BO servers are Auditees.

A CMS, which acts as an auditor, is both the auditor and the auditee.

Just in case the CMS is stopped, down, or loses connection to the Audit database, another CMS will take over the auditor role.

To identify which CMS in a BI cluster is an auditor, we can check the details on the CMC -> Auditing Page.

EVENTS

-The Audit database connection information, retention period, types of events to be audited, and additional required details—such as SQL statements for report refresh—are defined on the CMC -> Auditing page.

-Based on the selected events, the servers responsible for those events capture them in the form of a .txt file in the Auditing directory on their local machines.

-By default, the path for the Auditing directory, where intermediate auditing files are stored, is: C:\Program Files (x86)\SAP BusinessObjects\SAP BusinessObjects Enterprise XI 4.0\Auditing.

Naming Convention:

The naming convention follows the format: audit<EncodedServerName><Event_ID> (in hexadecimal form).

As a result, all files created by the same BO server will consistently begin with the same set of characters. Below is an example of a file name generated by auditing (note that the first five files all start with the same string, indicating they were generated by the same BI server).

Name	Date modified	Type	Size
audit8724a7653c62068618c1fc4c130c368...	7/5/2017 9:26 AM	Text Document	0 KB
audit8724a7653c62068618c1fc4c130c368...	7/24/2017 4:11 AM	Text Document	0 KB
audit8724a7653c62068618c1fc4c130c368...	5/12/2017 4:29 PM	Text Document	0 KB
audit8724a7653c62068618c1fc4c130c368...	5/15/2017 12:05 PM	Text Document	0 KB
audit8724a7653c62068618c1fc4c130c368...	8/21/2017 2:57 AM	Text Document	0 KB
audit44496d3a4ec385043982ac2f106a5ec...	7/6/2017 6:50 AM	Text Document	0 KB
audit44496d3a4ec385043982ac2f106a5ec...	7/24/2017 6:47 AM	Text Document	0 KB

Workflow in Detail:

i)-Each individual server will write its own auditing information into a temporary file on its local machine; these files can be found in the Auditing folder on each node.

ii)-The Auditor CMS maintains a list of all registered (running) servers.

iii)-This Auditor CMS sends a request to the first registered server in the list: "Send me any events that are currently waiting to be written to the Auditing Database."

iv)-The server acknowledges the request and then sends all the audit events and details that need to be written (the Auditee will read back the data in the auditing files it previously wrote in the Auditing folder).

v)-The servers, for example, the Webi processing server, look for each event from the .txt files and then send the details to the CMS in a structured format. All servers will send any event to the CMS using the same 'standard' structure.

vi)-The Auditor CMS then processes each of the events returned in order.

-If the event already exists in the auditing database, it is skipped, and the auditor moves on to the next event.

-The auditor checks whether the object related to the event (e.g. the refreshed Webi report or the user logging in) still exists in the CMS repository or if it has already been deleted.

-If the object is found in the CMS repository, the data is used to convert the CUID of the object (which is all that is stored when the audit event is written to the auditing folder) into the actual object name and folder path within BO.

Auditing Configuration:

Login to CMC using App or web server:

http://<Hostname>:8080/BOE/CMC using Enterprise Administrator credentials

Go to Auditing

Under configuration:

Check Use Windows Authentication and update Delete Events Older Than (Days) to 90 days.

Set the events to custom. Select the required fields > click on save

Restart all services (SIA) in order to take this effect on application servers.

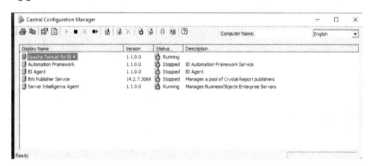

Chapter 9 CMC Configuration

Login to CMC > Application > right click on CMC and go to processing Settings >

Update the URL to common URL:

https://<BOServerName>/BOE/OpenDocument/opendo c/openDocument.jsp?sIDType=CUID&iDocID=%SI_CUI D%

to check opendoc:

https://<BOServerName>/BOE/OpenDocument/opendo c/openDocument.jsp?sType=wid&sRefresh=yes&sPath=[BOServer_Administrators]&sDocName=My_First_Audit +Report

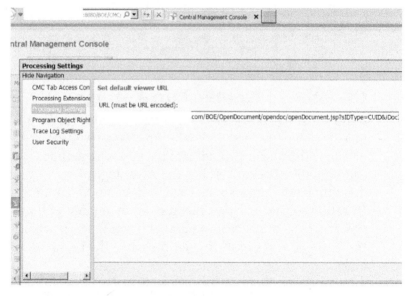

Go to program object rights >

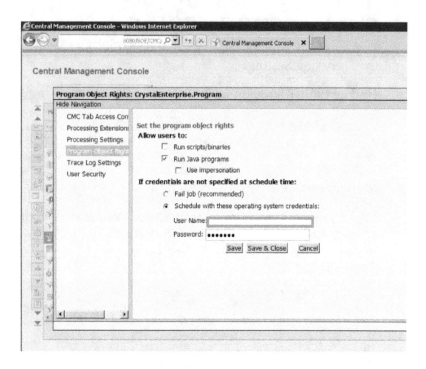

Chapter 10 Hot Backup settings

A hot backup is performed while the system is running and available to users, and data can change while the backup is being performed. Hot backup is sometimes called "online backup". It has the advantage of no downtime for your system. The Hot Backup Maximum Duration setting specifies the maximum amount of time that you expect the backup to take—from the time when the CMS backup begins to the time when the FRS backup ends.

Go to CMC - Settings - Hot Backup - Ensure Hot Backup is enabled and Legacy Applications Support is checked. Change Hot Backup maximum Duration to 720

Central Management Console

Settings ▾

▼ Properties

Data Source: BO_Repository
Database Name: ;bo_cmsrepo_test;microsoft sql server;13.00.5292
Database User Name: DUMMYTRUSTEDUSER
Auditing: Enabled

► View Global System Metrics

► Cluster

▼ Hot Backup

Enable Hot Backup: ☑
Hot Backup Maximum Duration (Minutes):   720
Enable Legacy Applications Support (Backup Limitations) ☑
Update

61

Chapter 11 User Attribute management settings:

Brief Explanation

A new feature available with BI 4.0 Feature Pack 3 is the ability to import and manage extended user attributes. This feature can be accessed in the Central Management Console (CMC). These extended attributes can be used for filtering and applying security at the universe (.unx) level.

For example, if your LDAP server has an attribute called "Country," you can utilise those values to filter content in your report based on the value of the Country attribute for any given user. Alternatively, you can set security so that someone from Canada cannot access content from Germany, and vice versa. The filtering and security will be set up using the Information Design Tool.

Let's explore a sample scenario

Let's say I have some users, one is located in the United States, and the other is in France. While I can represent this membership through user groups, in some cases, extended information such as region, country, and department can also be stored in your Active Directory or LDAP server. However, you may not always have groups configured to represent these extended attributes.

With BI4 Feature Pack 3, you can now reference and consume these extended attributes from your external identity stores, such as SAP, AD, and LDAP, as well as manage them directly for the BI 'enterprise' users. To do this, you must first configure your authentication plugin and enable the attribute binding options:

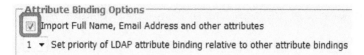

Attribute Binding Options
☑ Import Full Name, Email Address and other attributes
1 ▾ Set priority of LDAP attribute binding relative to other attribute bindings

Previously, this option allowed you to import the full name and email address, but we have now extended its functionality significantly.

Once you have enabled this setting, you will need to know the attribute names you wish to query. In this LDAP example, which is a screenshot from my LDAP server, I have an attribute called "Locality," which will be used for the country.

Allowed Attributes

First Name (givenname):

User ID (uid):   Jean-Luc

Password (userPassword):

Confirm Password:

E-mail (mail):

Telephone Number (telephoneNumber):

Fax Number (facsimileTelephoneNumber):

Locality (l):   France

To map this value to your users, click on the User Attribute Management link in the CMC

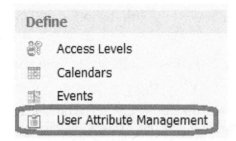

Define

- Access Levels
- Calendars
- Events
- **User Attribute Management**

Click on the "Add new Custom Mapped Attribute button"

In the screen presented to you, select the source of the attribute; in our case, this will be LDAP:

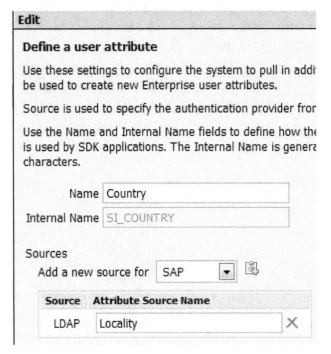

A brief explanation of the values.

The name will be used in all user interfaces where you interact with this in the BI tools.

The internal name is referenced by both the internal SDK and the Information Design Tool.

The Attribute Source name is the attribute value from our previously mentioned LDAP server.

Once this is done, you can run a user update in the LDAP authentication plugin or log on as one of the LDAP users to validate that your users have been updated with the appropriate values. For the various attribute sources to appear, the authentication plugin must be correctly configured and enabled. To validate this, check a user's properties page.

You can now see that the name we defined as "Country" holds the value from the LDAP server, which is stored under "Locality."

Great! So now what?!

Validation Scenario

Let's say I want Jean-Luc's reports to include only data for his region, France.

If I first log on to the Information Design Tool using the Jean-Luc user account and run a query on my universe with no filters, I'll get everything returned:

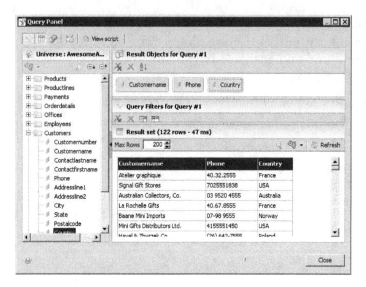

However, applying a filter based on country will limit my results to the value of the user's attribute:

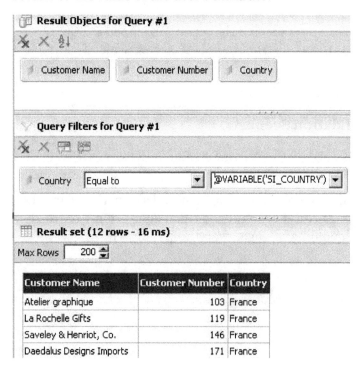

The value we input here is @VARIABLE('SI_COUNTRY') to utilise the custom mapped attributes. Recall that this is the internal name set when we created the attribute mapping in the CMC.

If we examine the details of our resulting query to understand what happens behind the scenes, we will see the following:

Where this becomes even more useful beyond filtering is in applying security. Suppose you don't want users to view data outside their region, as defined by the "Country" attribute in our example.

In the security builder of the Information Design Tool, insert a Data Security Profile:

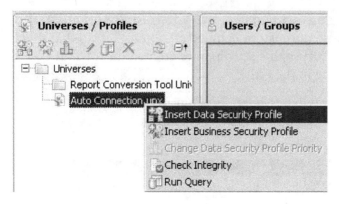

Let's now add a row-level security restriction on the Customers table.

Make sure to assign this security to an appropriate group. You can do this for 'Everyone' and then save your universe.

Now, if we log on again with our Jean-Luc user, whose 'Country' attribute value is "France", our query will always be limited to this value only, and I will not be able to access data for other countries.

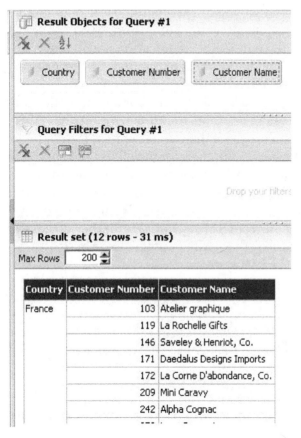

If Jean-Luc relocates to the USA, and assuming the underlying attribute is updated, their security access will be automatically updated as well, with their data filtered to "USA" only.

While the feature is primarily intended to leverage information from your existing Identity Provider, such as your LDAP directory store or Active Directory, it can also be applied to Enterprise users. Additionally, you can use the SDK to access and set these values.

Failover:

You will notice that you can set multiple attribute sources for a single custom attribute. For example, you can configure both your SAP authentication plugin and your AD plugin to pull in the value of Country. The priority of each source is defined during the authentication configuration. If a user has an alias for an authentication source, the system attempts to retrieve the attribute value from that source, even if the value is empty. If this attempt is unsuccessful, the system will use the next available source for which the user has an alias. In other words, if I have both SAP and AD configured, with SAP having priority, the value from AD will only be used if my user does not have an SAP user alias, or if they do have an SAP user alias but the attribute points to a non-existing attribute in the SAP system.

Steps:

Step 1) Go to CMC - User Attribute Management –

Step 2) Step 2) Click Add a New Custom Mapped Attribute - Enter the following attributes as the Name. The and the Attribute Source Name is after the dash (-):

Company - company

Job Title - title

Department - department

Office Location - physicaldeliveryofficename

Street Address - streetaddress

City - l

State/Province - st

Zip/Postal Code - postalcode

Country - co

Country Abbreviation - c

Telephone Number - telephoneNumber

Mobile Number - mobile

Assistant - msExchAssistantName

Assitant Phone - telephoneAssistant

Fax Number - facsimileTelephoneNumber

Soft Phone Number - otherTelephone

Phone Phone Number - homePhone

Pager Phone Number - pager

Last Name - sn

First name - givenName

Notes - info

Description - description

AD Account Codes - userAccountControl

ntral Management Console

Welcome: **Adminis**

User Attribute Management ▽

☐ ☐ ✕

Name	Internal Name	Source	Sources Attribute Source
Company	SI_COMPANY	Windows AD	Company
JobTitle	SI_JOBTITLE	Windows AD	title
Assistant	SI_ASSISTANT	Windows AD	msExchAssistantN
Last Name	SI_LASTNAME	Windows AD	sn
Pager Phone Number	SI_PAGERPHONENUMBER	Windows AD	pager
Phone Phone Number	SI_PHONEPHONENUMBER	Windows AD	homePhone
Description	SI_DESCRIPTION	Windows AD	description
Notes	SI_NOTES	Windows AD	info
Soft Phone Number	SI_SOFTPHONENUMBER	Windows AD	otherTelephone
Department	SI_DEPARTMENT	Windows AD	department
Office Location	SI_OFFICELOCATION	Windows AD	physicaldeliveryof
Street Address	SI_STREETADDRESS	Windows AD	streetaddress
Country Abbreviation	SI_COUNTRYABBREVIATION	Windows AD	c
Country	SI_COUNTRY	Windows AD	co
Zip/Postal Code	SI_ZIPPOSTALCODE	Windows AD	postalcode
AssitantPhone	SI_ASSITANTPHONE	Windows AD	telephoneAssistan
ADAccount Codes	SI_ADACCOUNTCODES	Windows AD	userAccountContr

SECTION 3 CONFIGURATIONS

Chapter 12 Windows AD Configuration

A directory is a hierarchical structure that stores information about objects on the network. A directory service, such as Active Directory Domain Services (AD DS), provides the methods for storing directory data and making this data available to network users and administrators. For example, AD DS stores information about user accounts, such as names, passwords, phone numbers, and so on, and enables other authorized users on the same network to access this information.

A Domain Controller (DC) allows the creation of logical containers. These containers consist of users, computers and groups. The Domain Controllers also help in organizing and managing the Servers.

Kerberos authentication is managed by a three-tiered system in which encrypted service tickets, rather than a plain-text user ID and password pair, are exchanged between the application server and client.

These encrypted service tickets, called credentials, are provided by a separate server called the Kerberos Key Distribution Center (KDC).

Credentials have a finite lifetime and are understood only by the client and the server. These features reduce the risk of a security exposure, even if the ticket is intercepted from the network. Each user, or principal in Kerberos terms, possesses a private encryption key that is shared with the KDC. Collectively, the principals and computers that are registered with a KDC are known as a realm

A Service Principal Name (SPN) is a unique identifier for a service instance. Kerberos authentication uses SPNs to associate a service instance with a service sign-in account. This allows a client application to request service authentication for an account, even if the client does not have the account name.

Step1)

Use the setspn -a command to add the service principal names (SPN) to the service account. Specify service principal names (SPNs) for the service account, as well as the server, fully qualified domain server and IP address for the machine on which BI launch pad is deployed.

Example:

Run the following command on the Active Directory server to create appropriate Service Principal Names (SPNs) by sending a mail to the AD team.

setspn –a BICMS/service_account_name.domain.com serviceaccountname

setspn -a HTTP/<servername> <servicename>

setspn -a HTTP/<servername.domain.com> <servicename>

BICMS is the name of the machine on which the SIA is running, <servername> is the name of the server on which BI launch pad is deployed and <servernamedomain> is its fully qualified domain name.

Change the user configuration of 'ServiceAccount' in Active Directory configuration, and under the Delegation tab, select "Trust this user for delegation to any service (Kerberos only)".

Change the user configuration of 'ServiceAccount' in Active Directory configuration, and under the Delegation tab, select "Trust this user for delegation to any service (Kerberos only)"

You need to setup AD account as below

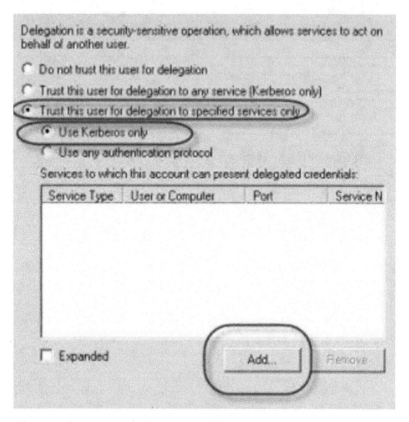

Change the user configuration of 'ServiceAccount' in Active Directory configuration, and under the Account tab, select "This account supports Kerberos AES 128 bit encryption" and ""This account supports Kerberos AES 256 bit encryption".

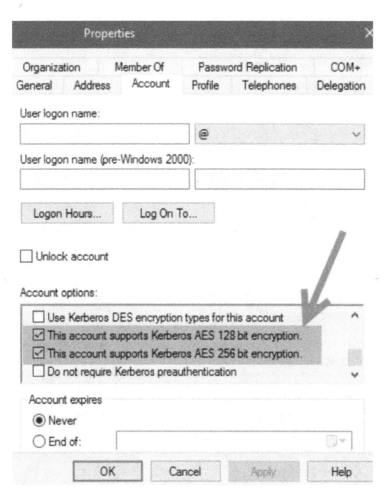

Step2)

CMC Configurations for Windows AD:

1. Login to CMC > Authentication > Windows AD

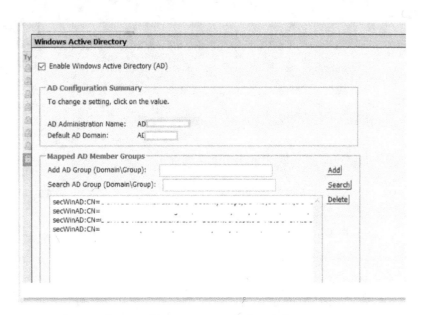

2. Enter the service account credentials

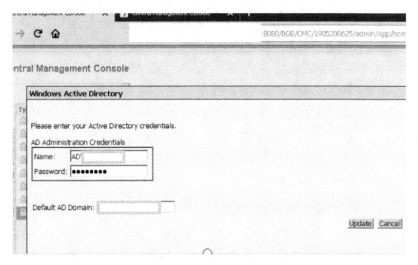

3. Update the SPN details
4. Import the windows AD groups
5. Schedule User's AD Alias Updates: set once in a day

6. Schedule AD Groups Updates: Set to run every 4 hours.

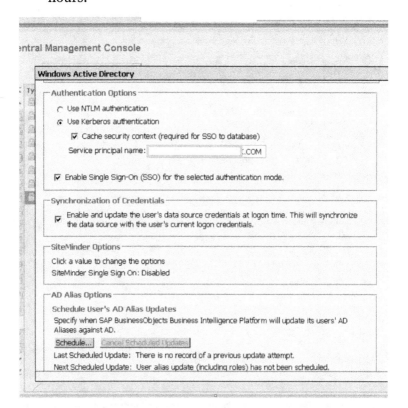

indows Active Directory

New Alias Options

- ⦿ Assign each new AD alias to an existing User Account with the same name
- ○ Create a new user account for each new AD alias

Alias Update Options

- ⦿ Create new aliases when the Alias Update occurs
- ○ Create new aliases only when a user logs on

New User Options

- ○ New users are created as named users
- ⦿ New users are created as concurrent users

─ Attribute Binding Options ──────────────────

☑ Import Full Name, Email Address and other attributes

[1 ▾] Set priority of AD attribute binding relative to other attribute bindings

─ AD Group Options ──────────────────────────

Schedule AD Groups Updates

Specify when SAP BusinessObjects Business Intelligence Platform will update its AD Groups.

[Schedule...] [Cancel Scheduled Updates]

Last Scheduled Update: There is no record of a previous update attempt.

Next Scheduled Update: Roles update has not been scheduled.

─ On-Demand AD Update ───────────────────────

- ○ Update AD Groups now
- ⦿ Update AD Groups and Aliases now
- ○ Do not update AD Groups and Aliases now

[Update] [Cance]

Schedule: Update Authentication Group Membership and User Aliase

Recurrence

Run object: | Daily   ⌄ |

Object will run once every N days.

Days(N) = | 1 |

Start Date/Time: | 08 ⌄ | 50 ⌄ | AM ⌄ | 5/30/2019 | ▦ |

End Date/Time: | 08 ⌄ | 50 ⌄ | AM ⌄ | 5/30/2029 | ▦ |

Once you add the AD groups, you should be able to see the users in Users & groups

Verify java can successfully receive a kerberos ticket:

The kinit command obtains or renews a Kerberos ticket-granting ticket.This tool is similar in functionality to the kinit tool that is commonly found in other Kerberos implementations.

E:\Program Files (x86)\SAP BusinessObjects\SAP BusinessObjects Enterprise XI 4.0\win64_x64\sapjvm\bin

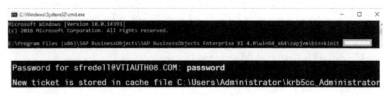

Step3)

Tomcat Configurations for Windows AD:

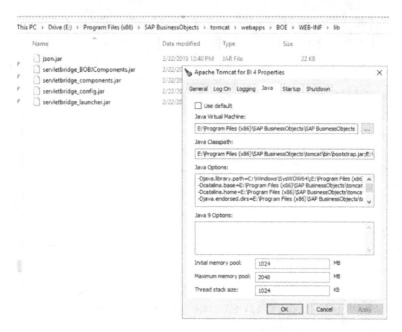

Add below lines at the end of the Java options:

-Djava.security.auth.login.config=C:/Windows/bscLogin.conf

-Djava.security.krb5.conf=C:/Windows/krb5.ini

Update max permsize to 1024M

-XX:MaxPermSize=1024M

Update the initial Memory Pool :

Maximum memory ppol:

Thread stack size:

Create files bscLogin.conf & krb5.ini under C:\Windows Directory

bscLogin.conf

krb5

Create a file named bscLogin.conf if it does not already exist, and store it in the C:\Windows directory.

Add the following code to the bscLogin.conf configuration file:

com.businessobjects.security.jgss.initiate {

com.sun.security.auth.module.Krb5LoginModule required debug=true;

};

```
com.businessobjects.security.jgss.initiate {
com.sun.security.auth.module.Krb5LoginModule required debug=true;
};|
```

Edit Krb5.ini file (You should open notepad in administrator mode then open krb5.ini file): the below Kerberos domain controller server names need to be updated following the next section.

[libdefaults]

default_realm = <add your organization domain>

dns_lookup_kdc = true

dns_lookup_realm = true

udp_preference_limit = 1

default_tgs_enctypes = rc4-hmac

default_tkt_enctypes = rc4-hmac

[realms]

<your organization domain name> = {

kdc = <Server 1>

kdc = <Server 2>

kdc = <Server 3>

kdc = <Server 4 based on number of servers>

default_domain = <your organization domain>

}

```
[libdefaults]
default_realm = <DOMAIN.COM>
dns_lookup_kdc = true
dns_lookup_realm = true
udp_preference_limit = 1
default_tgs_enctypes = rc4-hmac
default_tkt_enctypes = rc4-hmac
[realms]
<DOMAIN.COM> = {
kdc = <HOSTNAME.DOMAIN.COM>
kdc = <HOSTNAME1.DOMAIN.COM>
kdc = <HOSTNAME2.DOMAIN.COM>
kdc = <HOSTNAME3.DOMAIN.COM>
default_domain = <DOMAIN.COM>
}
```

Another example of krb5.ini

[libdefaults]

default_realm = ATHENA.MIT.EDU

[realms]

  ATHENA.MIT.EDU = {

    kdc = kerberos.mit.edu

    kdc = kerberos-1.mit.edu

    admin_server = kerberos.mit.edu

  }

WebiSample folder import:

Step 1: To import WebiSamples, go to the below mentioned path:

E:\Program Files (x86)\SAP BusinessObjects\SAP BusinessObjects Enterprise XI 4.0\Samples\webi

Step2: Copy the WebiSamples.lcmbiar file and import into environment as follows

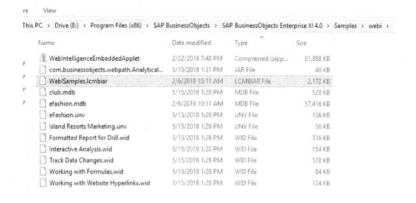

BI LunchPad

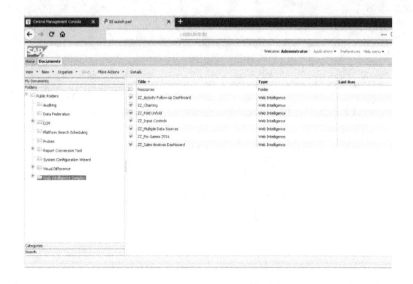

Chapter 13 Single Sign on Configuration

SSO has explained below, perhaps you are an administrator for your company which has two Oracle Cloud services and you must provision these services to your company's organization, roles, and users. Your company may also have on-premise applications and cloud services from other vendors. It's important that communication between these services and applications is done in a secure fashion. With SSO, users can sign in to all of them using the same set of credentials that are managed by using your identity domain system. In other terms Single Sign-On application enables users to log in once to gain secure access to all the software they require throughout the day with no need to log in again.

Key benefits

Increased user productivity:

Simplify your users' everyday work and boost employee productivity by eliminating the need to perform separate log in procedures for each business application.

Higher profits from increased cost efficiency:

Lower your help desk costs with a significant reduction in support calls focused on recovering passwords and unlocking accounts.

Greater security:

Implement powerful security measures for your business-critical applications by using risk-based and two-factor authentication.

All Kerberos server machines need a keytab file to authenticate to the KDC. The keytab file should be readable only by root, and should exist only on the machine's local disk. The file should not be part of any backup of the machine, unless access to the backup data is secured as tightly as access to the machine's root password.

Generate using below command on DC end with the below command and copy that file file in C:\Windows directory

Step1)

ktpass out C:/windows/host.keytab princ <serviceAccount>@<DomainName> pass **** kvno 255 ptype KRB5_NT_PRINCIPAL crypto RC4-HMAC-NT

Go to F:\Program Files (x86)\SAP BusinessObjects\tomcat\webapps\BOE\WEB-INF\config\custom

Copy the 3 configuration files (BIlaunchpad.properties, OpenDocument.properties & global.properties)

Step2)

Edit **global.properties** file

Ensure idm.princ has correct service account as below

 idm.princ= <ServiceAccount Name>

the updated entries should be like below:

sso.enabled=true

siteminder.enabled=false

vintela.enabled=true

idm.realm=<DomainName>

idm.princ=<ServiceName>

idm.keytab=C:/windows/host.keytab

idm.allowUnsecured=true

idm.allowNTLM=false

idm.logger.name=simple

idm.logger.props=error-log.properties

```
sso.enabled=true
siteminder.enabled=false
vintela.enabled=true
idm.realm=<Domain Name>
idm.princ=<Service Account Name>|
idm.keytab=C:/windows/host.keytab
idm.allowUnsecured=true
idm.allowNTLM=false
idm.logger.name=simple
idm.logger.props=error-log.properties
```

Step3)

Edit **BILaunchpad.properties** file and ensure the cms name is updated correctly as below

cms.default= <CMS Name>:6400

Step4)

Edit **OpenDocument.propertie**s file and ensure cms name is updated correctly as below:

cms.default= <CMS Name>:6400

Step5)

server.xml configuration:

Take backup of server.xml file from F:\Program Files (x86)\SAP BusinessObjects\tomcat\conf

Edit server.xml file to make sure httpheader size is set to 65536 like below

```
<Connector port="8080" protocol="HTTP/1.1"
connectionTimeout="20000" redirectPort="8443"
compression="on" URIEncoding="UTF-8"
compressionMinSize="2048"
noCompressionUserAgents="gozilla, traviata"
compressableMimeType="text/html,text/xml,text/plain,t
ext/css,text/javascript,text/json,application/json"
maxHttpHeaderSize="65536"/>
```

save all files & Restart Tomcat to take effect this SSO.

Chapter 14 SSL Configuration

An SSL certificate is a digital certificate that verifies a website's identity and facilitates an encrypted connection. SSL, which stands for Secure Sockets Layer, is a security protocol that establishes a secure, encrypted link between a web server and a web browser. Companies and organizations must implement SSL certificates on their websites to secure online transactions and protect customer information. SSL enables secure communication between the web server and the browser by creating a protected transmission tunnel, which helps prevent eavesdropping.

Since its inception around 25 years ago, multiple versions of the SSL protocol have encountered security issues at various times. This led to the development of a revamped and renamed version known as TLS (Transport Layer Security), which remains in use today. However, the original initials SSL have persisted, and the updated protocol is still commonly referred to by its predecessor's name.

SSL (Secure Sockets Layer) and its successor, TLS (Transport Layer Security), are protocols designed to establish secure connections between networked computers.

How do SSL certificates work?

SSL ensures that any data transferred between users and websites, or between two systems, remains unreadable. It employs encryption algorithms to scramble data during transit, preventing hackers from intercepting and reading it as it travels over the connection. This data may include sensitive information such as names, addresses, credit card numbers, and other financial details.

When a website is secured by an SSL certificate, the acronym HTTPS (HyperText Transfer Protocol Secure) appears in the URL. If there is no SSL certificate, only HTTP will be shown, lacking the S for Secure. Additionally, a padlock icon will be displayed in the URL address bar, signaling trust and providing reassurance to website visitors.

Steps has to be required as below.

>> Generate key and certificate files for every machine in your deployment.

SSL configuration should be performed exclusively on WEB Servers, following this order:

To configure the BI platform Tomcat to use HTTPS, follow these steps on the machine where the BI platform is installed..

Step 1) keystore and certificate creation

Generating <Keystore Name>.jks file

Open command prompt and go to F:\Program Files (x86)\SAP BusinessObjects\SAP BusinessObjects Enterprise XI 4.0\win64_x64\sapjvm\bin

Use the following command only once per server; it creates the certificate KeyStore.

keytool -genkey -alias server -keyalg RSA -keystore <Keystore Name>.jks

You should see a couple of prompts after running the command above. Please follow the instructions below to fill in those prompts.

Use the domain name as both the first name and the last name.

Refer to the table below for the first and last names corresponding to each environment you are configuring.

Host Name: - <HostName>

Use the first part of your URL as the Organizational Unit, adding a number at the end if it is an additional server.

Follow below table for name of organizational unit:

<Organization Name TEST>: IT&S

Use the major city near which the server is located as the city. <City or Locality>

Use the fully spelled-out name of the state or province in which the city is located. <State or Province>

Use the two-letter code for the country in which the state or province is located. <US>

Type yes if everything is correct. The string should look similar to this:

Is CN= <HostName>.local, OU= IT&S, O=<OrganizationName>, L= <StateName1>, ST=<StateName2>, C=<CountryName> correct? [no]: yes

type the administrator password one more time

Please see the screen print for the ready reference.

Once you've executed all the above commands, you should see <Keystore Name>.jks file in the F:\Program Files (x86)\SAP BusinessObjects\SAP BusinessObjects Enterprise XI 4.0\win64_x64\sapjvm\bin directory.

Step2) Generate certificate signing request (CSR) using the keystore generated in previous steps

Generating csr.txt

To request a new SSL certificate:

Open command prompt and Go to F:\Program Files\Business Objects\j2sdk1.4.2_08\bin

Type the below command to delete any existing csr.txt files.

del /q csr.txt

If the csr.txt does not exist then ignore the above Del command.

Type the below command to generate csr.txt file

keytool -certreq -alias server -file csr.txt -keystore <KeystorName>.jks

```
Warning:
The JKS keystore uses a proprietary format. It is recommended to migrate to PKCS12 which is an industry standard format
using "keytool -importkeystore -srckeystore ████.jks -destkeystore ████.jks -deststoretype pkcs12".

E:\Program Files (x86)\SAP BusinessObjects\SAP BusinessObjects Enterprise XI 4.0\win64_x64\sapjvm\bin>del /q csr.txt

E:\Program Files (x86)\SAP BusinessObjects\SAP BusinessObjects Enterprise XI 4.0\win64_x64\sapjvm\bin>keytool -certreq -
alias server -file csr.txt -keystore ████.jks
Enter keystore password:

Warning:
The JKS keystore uses a proprietary format. It is recommended to migrate to PKCS12 which is an industry standard format
using "keytool -importkeystore -srckeystore ████.jks -destkeystore ████.jks -deststoretype pkcs12".

E:\Program Files (x86)\SAP BusinessObjects\SAP BusinessObjects Enterprise XI 4.0\win64_x64\sapjvm\bin>
```

Use the Administrator password as your keystore
password

Use the csr.txt file in your request for a new SSL
certificate

**Step3) Sign it from CA authority -the certificate
signing request generated in the previous steps
should be signed by the CA authority of your
organization for eg.. as mentioned below or using
any 3rd party tool.**

Requesting SSL Certificates

Send an email to Digital ID's, attaching the csr.txt file and
the required information. These details are needed by the
team.

Mail Subject: Request SSL Certificate

*To obtain a certificate, we require the following
information:*

a) Requesters Name -

b) Requesters Email address -

c) Application Department/Segment -

d) Organization Contact Name -

e) Team/Support mailbox email address -

f) The Web Server's platform (Apache, Microsoft, etc.) -

g) CMS (Atrium) ID number of the Application the certificate is required for -

h) Description of the web site/application –

- *Internal or External facing -*
- *Type of users (Organization users with Organization built machines/non-organization build machines) –*

i) A certificate signing request (CSR) -

Step4) Install Certificates:

When you receive the new certificate files from the SSL certificate team, please place them in the following directory. (F:\Program Files (x86)\SAP BusinessObjects\SAP BusinessObjects Enterprise XI 4.0\win64_x64\sapjvm\bin).

You should get three certificates from Digital Ids' called root.cer.txt, intermediate.cer.txt and <domain name>.cer.txt.

If the certificates are attached, you can download them from the email.

Copy the three files to the location specified below.

F:\Program Files (x86)\SAP BusinessObjects\SAP BusinessObjects Enterprise XI 4.0\win64_x64\sapjvm\bin

Adding Root certificate

Open command prompt and go to F:\Program Files
(x86)\SAP BusinessObjects\SAP BusinessObjects
Enterprise XI 4.0\win64_x64\sapjvm\bin

And run the following command to install root certificate.

**keytool -import -trustcacerts -alias root -file
root.cer -keystore <FileName>.jks**

enter the administrator password and tell it to trust the
certificate

You should get a confirmation stating that the Certificate
was installed in keystore.

Adding Intermediate certificate

Open command prompt and go to F:\Program Files
(x86)\SAP BusinessObjects\SAP BusinessObjects
Enterprise XI 4.0\win64_x64\sapjvm\bin

And run the following command to install intermediate
certificate.

**keytool -import -trustcacerts -alias intermediate -
file intermediate.cer -keystore <FileName>.jks**

enter the administrator password

You should get a confirmation stating that the Certificate was installed in keystore

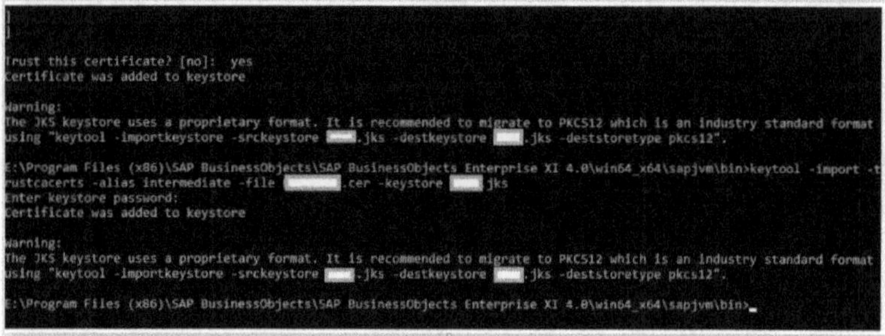

Adding the Domain certificate

Open command prompt and go to F:\Program Files (x86)\SAP BusinessObjects\SAP BusinessObjects Enterprise XI 4.0\win64_x64\sapjvm\bin

And run the following command to install domain (main) certificate.

keytool -import -trustcacerts -alias server -file <ServerName>.cer -keystore <FileName>.jks

enter the administrator password and tell it to trust the certificate

You should get a confirmation stating that the Certificate was installed in keystore

Please refer the following screen print for reference.

```
Certificate was added to keystore

Warning:
The JKS keystore uses a proprietary format. It is recommended to migrate to PKCS12 which is an industry standard format
using "keytool -importkeystore -srckeystore ████.jks -destkeystore ████.jks -deststoretype pkcs12".

E:\Program Files (x86)\SAP BusinessObjects\SAP BusinessObjects Enterprise XI 4.0\win64_x64\sapjvm\bin>keytool -import -t
rustcacerts -alias server -file ████████ cer  -keystore ████.jks
Enter keystore password:
Certificate reply was installed in keystore

Warning:
The JKS keystore uses a proprietary format. It is recommended to migrate to PKCS12 which is an industry standard format
using "keytool -importkeystore -srckeystore ████.jks -destkeystore ████.jks -deststoretype pkcs12".

E:\Program Files (x86)\SAP BusinessObjects\SAP BusinessObjects Enterprise XI 4.0\win64_x64\sapjvm\bin>
```

99

SECTION 4 SERVER CONFIGURATIONS

Chapter 15 Session Time out

You need to modify the web.xml file located in the WEB-INF directory of your web application to update the session timeout settings. Please edit the web.xml file only on the web server.

F:\Program Files (x86)\SAP BusinessObjects\tomcat\webapps\BOE\WEB-INF

Find: <session-timeout>20</session-timeout>

Replace with below:

<session-timeout>120</session-timeout>

Similarly, open the files located in the paths below and update the session timeout to 120.

Open F:\Program Files (x86)\SAP
BusinessObjects\tomcat\webapps\explorer\WEB-
INF\web.xml and change the session-timeout to 120

Open F:\Program Files (x86)\SAP
BusinessObjects\tomcat\webapps\
\AdminTools\WEB_INF\web.xml and change the
session-timeout to 120

Open
Tomcat\webapps\MobileBIService\WEB_INF\web.xml
and change the session-timeout to 120

Chapter 16 Tomcat users xml Configuration

Access control for the Tomcat Manager and Host
Manager involves defining user roles, along with
corresponding usernames and passwords, and assigning
these roles to users as part of Tomcat's built-in security
mechanisms.

In tomcat-users.xml file and update the administrator
password with appropriate environment:

Ex: Ensure password is updated to appropriate
environments:

<user username="administrator" password="****"/>

```
<!--
  <role rolename="tomcat"/>
  <role rolename="role1"/>
  <user username="tomcat" password="<must-be-changed>" roles="tomcat"/>
  <user username="both" password="<must-be-changed>" roles="tomcat,role1"/>
  <role rolename="manager-gui"/>
  <user username="administrator" password="must-be-changed" roles="manager-gui"/>
  <user username="role1" password="<must-be-changed>" roles="role1"/>
-->
</tomcat-users>
```

Restart the Tomcat on APP & Web

Manual Windows AD should be working now.

Chapter 17 DNS Configuration

The Domain Name System (DNS) is the phonebook of the Internet.

The Domain Name System (DNS) acts as the Internet's phonebook. People access information online using domain names, such as nytimes.com or espn.com, while web browsers communicate using Internet Protocol (IP) addresses. DNS translates these domain names into IP addresses, enabling browsers to load Internet resources efficiently.

Each device connected to the Internet is assigned a unique IP address, which allows other machines to locate it. DNS servers simplify this process by removing the necessity for humans to remember IP addresses, whether they are the simpler numerical formats like 192.168.1.1 (IPv4) or the more complex alphanumeric addresses such as 2400:cb00:2048:1::c629:d7a2 (IPv6).

How does DNS work?

The process of DNS resolution involves converting a hostname (such as www.example.com) into a computer-friendly IP address (such as 192.168.1.1).

Send an email to your Organisation's DNS Administrator team using the format provided below, as per your organisation's guidelines:

Admin,

Please create the following internal URL for the <BO environment> used by users on the <organization> network.

Scheduled Date	Scheduled Time
DD-MM-YYYY	HH:MM AM CST/IST

DNS Zone name (Domain name)	Add / Delete?	Host Name	Record Type	Target	Process reverse entry?	Internal/External / Both
<Server Name>	**Add**	<host Name Dev>	**Cname**	<Server Name>	**NO**	**Internal**
<server Name>	**Add**	<Host Name Prrod>	**Cname**	<Server Name>	**NO**	**Internal**

Chapter 18 Server.xml configuration with NIO settings

Explanation of the Most Commonly Used Tomcat Directories.

Tomcat directories

/bin:

It includes startup, shutdown, and other scripts.

/conf:

It contains configuration files, with the most important being server.xml.

/logs:

By default, log files are stored here.

/webapps:

This is where your web applications are stored.

/work :

A directory that holds temporary working directories for deployed web applications.

/temp :

A directory used by the JVM to store temporary files.

Tomcat parameters

CATALINA_HOME:

It is a Tomcat installation directory, for example, C:\Program Files\tomcat

CATALINA_BASE:

To To run multiple Tomcat instances on a single machine, to configure specific tomcat instance at runtime by using the CATALINA_BASE .

Note: By default, CATALINA_HOME and CATALINA_BASE direct to the same directory.

Element structure in server.xml as Server>Listener > GlobalNamingResources >Service >Executor>Connector >Engine >Host >Realm and their explanation as below

Server:

Represents the entire Catalina servlet container. A server must be assigned a shutdown port number.

Listener:

Typically used for starting or stopping Tomcat.

GlobalNamingResources:

The server's global JNDI resources are usually located in the tomcat-users.xml file.

Service:

The combination of one or more Connectors that use a single Engine to process incoming requests. Additionally, one or more Service elements may be nested within a Server element.

Executor:

A thread pool that can be shared among components in Tomcat is defined as a nested element within the Service element. To ensure the connectors recognise it, the Executor element must be placed before the Connector element in the server.xml file.

Connector:

Receive the request through a specified protocol Engine. This includes the complete request processing system associated with a particular Catalina Service. It handles all requests from one or more Connectors. An Engine MUST be nested within a Service element, following all related Connector elements associated with that Service.

Host:

Within this Engine element, each Host represents a different virtual host associated with the server. At least one Host is required, and one of the nested Hosts must have a name that matches the name specified for the defaultHost attribute.

Realm:

a "database" of usernames, passwords, and roles assigned to those users, similar to Unix groups.

The server.xml file in Tomcat is used to define and configure HTTP/HTTPS connectors, set up SSL/TLS, and integrate with LDAP and Active Directory.

Step1)

Take a backup of the server.xml file, then edit the server.xml file from F:\Program Files (x86)\SAP BusinessObjects\tomcat\conf \server.xml

The following line should already exist at the specified path.

```
<Connector port="8080" protocol="HTTP/1.1"
connectionTimeout="20000" redirectPort="8443"
```

```
compression="on" URIEncoding="UTF-8"
compressionMinSize="2048"
noCompressionUserAgents="gozilla, traviata"
compressableMimeType="text/html,text/xml,text/plain,t
ext/css,text/javascript,text/json,application/json"
maxHttpHeaderSize="65536"/>
```

Paste the following line directly after the code provided above.

code

Path:

F:\Program Files (x86)\SAP BusinessObjects\SAP
BusinessObjects Enterprise XI 4.0\win64_x64\sapjvm\bin

```
<Connector URIEncoding="UTF-8" acceptCount="100"
connectionTimeout="7200000"
disableUploadTimeout="true" enableLookups="false"
SSLEnabled="true" maxHttpHeaderSize="65535"
maxSpareThreads="75" maxThreads="1024"
minSpareThreads="25" port="443" scheme="https"
secure="true" clientAuth="false" sslProtocol="TLS"
keyAlias="server" keystoreFile="F:\Program Files
(x86)\SAP BusinessObjects\SAP BusinessObjects
Enterprise XI
4.0\win64_x64\sapjvm\bin\<FileName>.jks"
keystorePass="*******"
protocol="org.apache.coyote.http11.Http11NioProtocol"/
>
```

```
<Connector port="80" connectionTimeout="20000"
redirectPort="443"
```

protocol="org.apache.coyote.http11.Http11NioProtocol"/
>

Enter the administrator password in the keystorePass
field.

Restart Tomcat: The restart will take longer than 10 minutes.

Step 2)

Configuring Root Directory:

In the ROOT folder, find the path below where the images and
index.htm pages are stored.

F:\Program Files (x86)\SAP
BusinessObjects\tomcat\webapps\ROOT

Chapter 19 Default CMS name update

We need to update the default CMS name in both the
CMC and BI Launchpad screens. This update should only
be carried out on web servers.

Go to F:\Program Files (x86)\SAP
BusinessObjects\tomcat\webapps\BOE\WEB-
INF\config\default

Edit the CmcApp.properties and BIlaunchpad.properties
files, updating the cms.default entry to reflect the
appropriate CMS names.

Ex:

cms.default= <HostName>:6400

Chapter 20 SMTPfrom settings

While scheduling the reports in the "From" field, you can choose to hide it so that it is not visible to the user scheduling the report. In this case, the "From" address will be taken from the report's default settings or the job server. To achieve this, set SMTPFrom to false.

Apply the settings to released inactive sessions. To achieve this, set logontoken.enabled to false.

Modify F:\Program Files (x86)\SAP BusinessObjects\tomcat\webapps\BOE\WEB-INF\config\custom\BIlaunchpad.properties & OpenDocument.properties file

Add SMTPFrom=false

Add logontoken.enabled=false

Chapter 21 Tomcat Persistent Session Manager

In SAP BusinessObjects (BO), the Tomcat Persistent Session Manager settings pertain to how Apache Tomcat (the default application server for SAP BO) handles user sessions. Persistent sessions allow for user session data to be stored across server restarts, enabling users to resume their sessions without losing state or being forced to log in again.

Open `conf/context.xml` and ensure the following lines are not commented out:

```
<Manager pathname="" />


<!--

  <Manager pathname="" />

  -->


Change to

  <Manager pathname="" />
```

SECTION 5 ADD ON INSTALLATIONS

Chapter 22 Analysis for Office

Stop all the services except 3 of the services of CMS, OFRS and IFRS in CMC

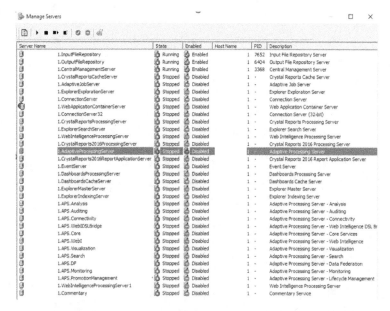

Go to the setup, right-click on it, and select 'Run as administrator.'

Select setup language as 'English' and then click 'ok'

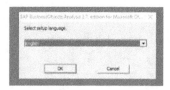

Click 'Next'

Click 'Next'

Click 'Next'

I Accept the license agreement option

Click 'Next'

Select Full Installation Option

Provide Server CMS Name and Port in 'Connection Information for Existing CMS'

Provide password for Administrator in 'CMS Administrator Login Information'

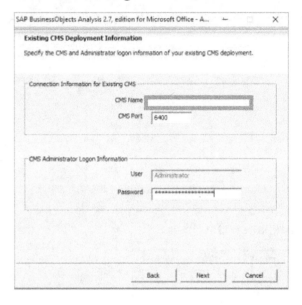

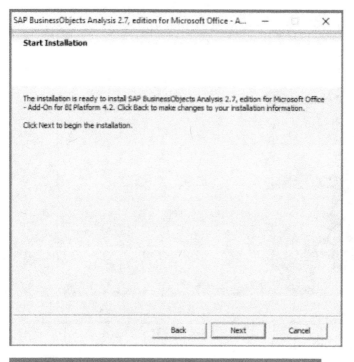

Start Installation

The installation is ready to install SAP BusinessObjects Analysis 2.7, edition for Microsoft Office - Add-On for BI Platform 4.2. Click Back to make changes to your installation information.

Click Next to begin the installation.

Back   Next   Cancel

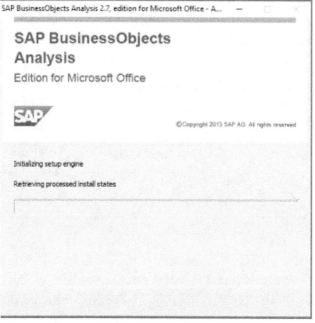

SAP BusinessObjects Analysis

Edition for Microsoft Office

© Copyright 2013 SAP AG. All rights reserved

Initializing setup engine

Retrieving processed install states

Click 'Finish'

After completing the installation, log in to CMC and enable all the services.

Login to BI Launchpad and make sure you are able to refresh the reports by verifying couple of reports as part of validation.

Chapter 23 Explorer Addon Installation

Stop all the services except 3 of the services of CMS, OFRS and IFRS in CMC

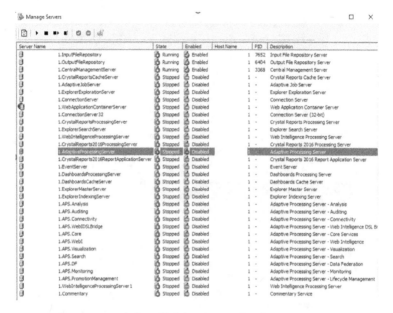

Go to the setup, right-click on it, and select 'Run as administrator.'

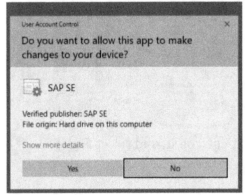

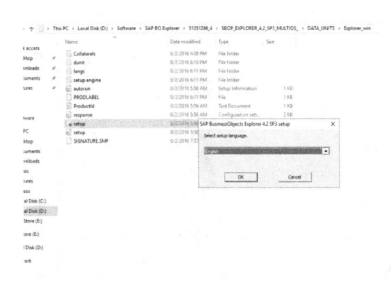

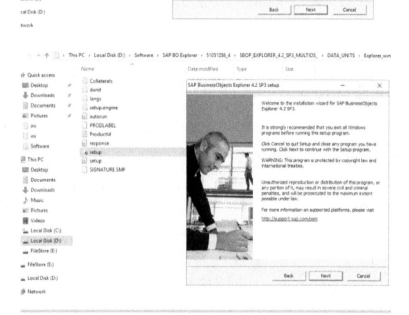

Home   Share   View   Manage

← ↑ 📁 › This PC › Local Disk (D:) › Software › SAP BO Explorer › 51051286_4 › SBOP_EXPLORER_4.2_SP3_MULTIOS_ › DATA_UNITS › Explorer_win

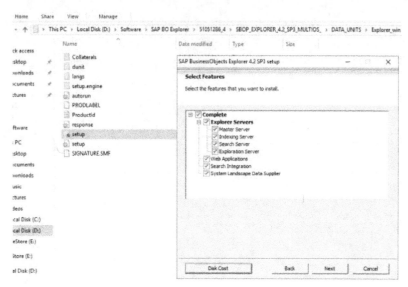

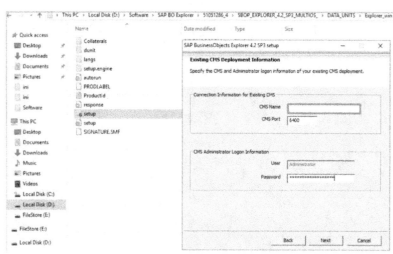

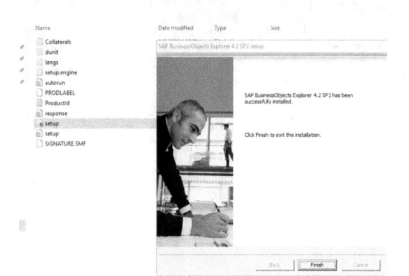

Name	Date modified	Type	Size
Collaterals			
dunit			
langs			
setup.engine			
autorun			
PRODLABEL			
ProductId			
response			
setup			
setup			
SIGNATURE.SMF			

SAP BusinessObjects Explorer 4.2 SP3 setup

SAP BusinessObjects Explorer 4.2 SP3 has been successfully installed.

Click Finish to exit this installation.

Back   Finish   Cancel

Chapter 24 Design Studio Addon Installation

Stop all the services except 3 of the services of CMS, OFRS and IFRS in CMC.

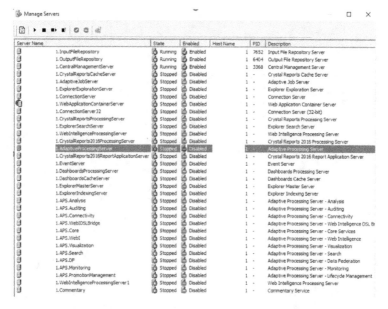

Go to the setup, right-click on it, and select 'Run as administrator.'

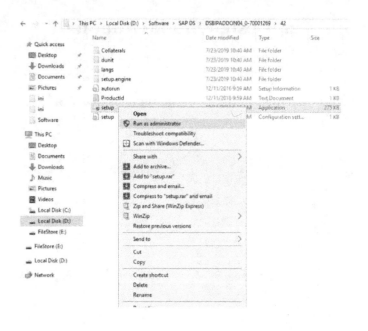

Welcome to the installation wizard for SAP BusinessObjects Design Studio 1.6 for BI Platform 4.2.

It is strongly recommended that you exit all Windows programs before running this setup program.

Click Cancel to quit Setup and close any program you have running. Click Next to continue with the Setup program.

WARNING: This program is protected by copyright law and international treaties.

Unauthorized reproduction or distribution of this program, or any portion of it, may result in severe civil and criminal penalties, and will be prosecuted to the maximum extent possible under law.

PC > Local Disk (D:) > Software > SAP DS > DSBIPADDON04_0-70001269 > 42

Name	Date modified	Type	Size
Collaterals			
dunit			
langs			
setup.engine			
autorun			
ProductId			
setup			
setup			

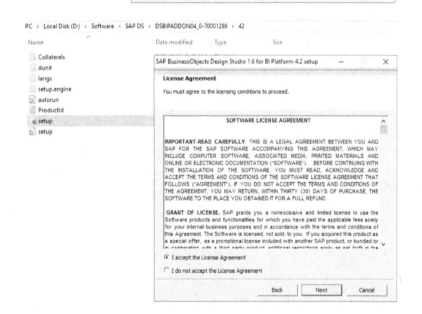

SAP BusinessObjects Design Studio 1.6 for BI Platform 4.2 setup

License Agreement

You must agree to the licensing conditions to proceed.

SOFTWARE LICENSE AGREEMENT

IMPORTANT-READ CAREFULLY: THIS IS A LEGAL AGREEMENT BETWEEN YOU AND SAP FOR THE SAP SOFTWARE ACCOMPANYING THIS AGREEMENT, WHICH MAY INCLUDE COMPUTER SOFTWARE, ASSOCIATED MEDIA, PRINTED MATERIALS AND ONLINE OR ELECTRONIC DOCUMENTATION ("SOFTWARE"). BEFORE CONTINUING WITH THE INSTALLATION OF THE SOFTWARE, YOU MUST READ, ACKNOWLEDGE AND ACCEPT THE TERMS AND CONDITIONS OF THE SOFTWARE LICENSE AGREEMENT THAT FOLLOWS ("AGREEMENT"). IF YOU DO NOT ACCEPT THE TERMS AND CONDITIONS OF THE AGREEMENT, YOU MAY RETURN, WITHIN THIRTY (30) DAYS OF PURCHASE, THE SOFTWARE TO THE PLACE YOU OBTAINED IT FOR A FULL REFUND.

GRANT OF LICENSE. SAP grants you a nonexclusive and limited license to use the Software products and functionalities for which you have paid the applicable fees solely for your internal business purposes and in accordance with the terms and conditions of this Agreement. The Software is licensed, not sold, to you. If you acquired this product as a special offer, as a promotional license included with another SAP product, or bundled or in combination with a third party product, additional restrictions apply as set forth in the

(•) I accept the License Agreement

(○) I do not accept the License Agreement

Back   Next   Cancel

130

Name	Date modified	Type	Size
Collaterals			
dunit			
langs			
setup.engine			
autorun			
ProductId			
setup			
setup			

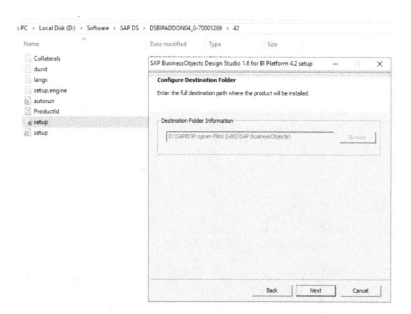

SAP BusinessObjects Design Studio 1.6 for BI Platform 4.2 setup   —   ☐   ✕

Configure Destination Folder

Enter the full destination path where the product will be installed.

Destination Folder Information

D:\SAPBI\Program Files (x86)\SAP BusinessObjects\   Browse

Back   Next   Cancel

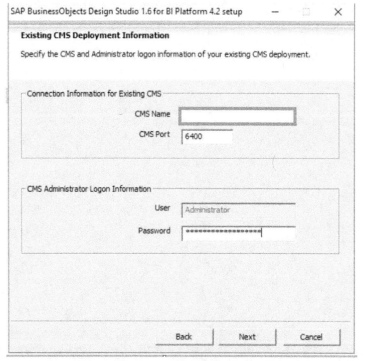

SAP BusinessObjects Design Studio 1.6 for BI Platform 4.2 setup   —   ☐   ✕

Existing CMS Deployment Information

Specify the CMS and Administrator logon information of your existing CMS deployment.

Connection Information for Existing CMS

CMS Name   [   ]

CMS Port   6400

CMS Administrator Logon Information

User   Administrator

Password   ********************

Back   Next   Cancel

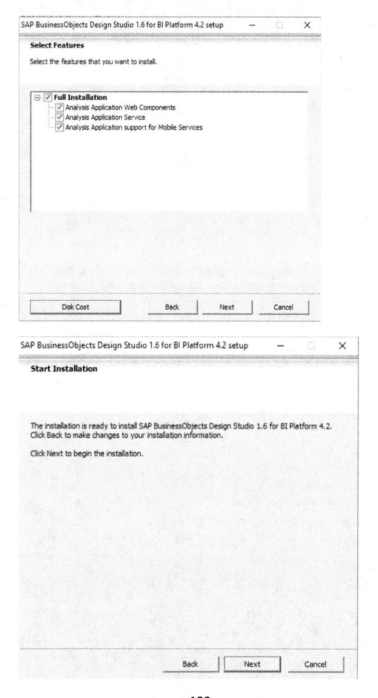

SAP BusinessObjects Design Studio 1.6 for BI Platform 4.2 setup — ☐ ✕

Post Installation Steps

Installation is complete. Follow the post installation instructions below to complete your deployment.

Post Installation Instructions:

- BI Platform web applications have been affected by this installation. If you have multiple Web application server nodes or if you are not using the default Tomcat or Web Application Container Service (WACS), you might need use the WDeploy tool to manually deploy Web applications to all your Web application server nodes. For more information, see the Web Application Deployment Guide on the SAP Help Portal at http://help.sap.com/bobip42.

Back   Next   Cancel

SECTION 6 UPGRADATION

Chapter 25 Upgrade Activity

This chapter is related only to Upgradation. If your project is not related to Upgradation, you can skip this chapter. Once the Server is installed, we need to copy the Source system CMS Database into the Target system CMS Database. To do this, we must follow the steps outlined below. After the CMS Database has been copied successfully, we will need to recreate the Node in the new Server CMS, as it currently contains only the old system Node services.

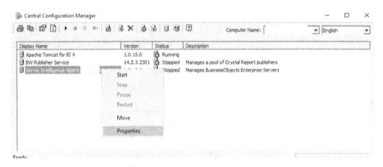

Click on 'Specify' to copy the Original Source System CMS Database to the newly installed Server CMS Database, and then select the option 'Copy data from another data source'.

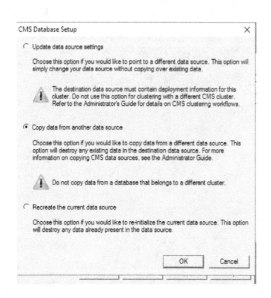

To provide the Source system CMS database details, click the 'Specify' tab. For the Target system CMS database details, click the 'Browse' tab.

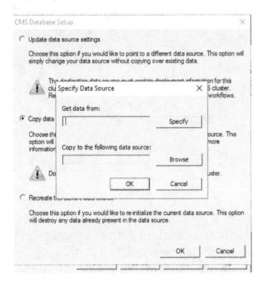

Select SQL Server (ODBC) as the source system, as SQL Server is the system being used in my scenario.

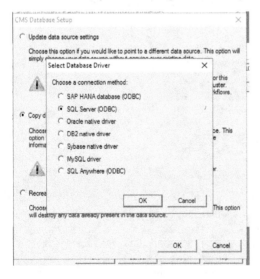

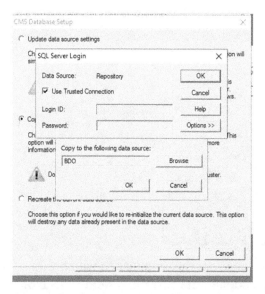

Select the database from which you want to copy. Ensure that the current system account has read access to the source database.

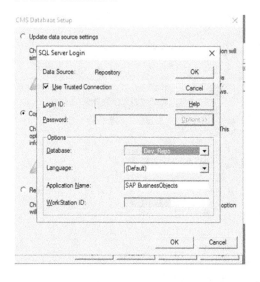

137

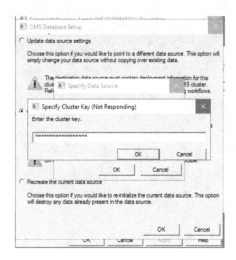

By clicking "Browse," select the database to which the data should be copied, i.e., the current system CMS DB.

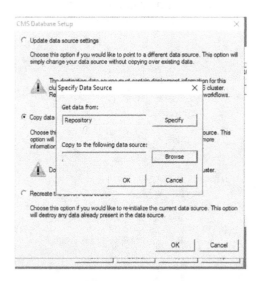

Ensure that you have correctly chosen the source and target systems. If you are confident that they are correct, then click 'Yes'.

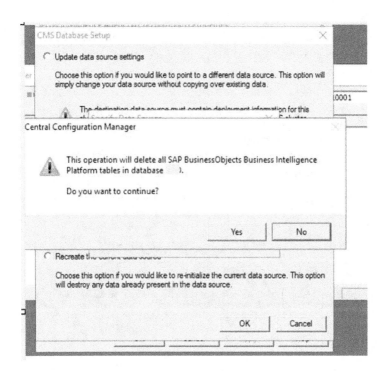

CMS Database Setup ✕

☐ Update data source settings

Choose this option if you would like to point to a different data source. This option will simply change your data source without copying over existing data.

⚠ The destination data source must contain deployment information for this

0001

Central Configuration Manager ✕

⚠ This operation will delete all SAP BusinessObjects Business Intelligence Platform tables in database).

Do you want to continue?

Yes | No

☐ Recreate the current data source

Choose this option if you would like to re-initialize the current data source. This option will destroy any data already present in the data source.

OK | Cancel

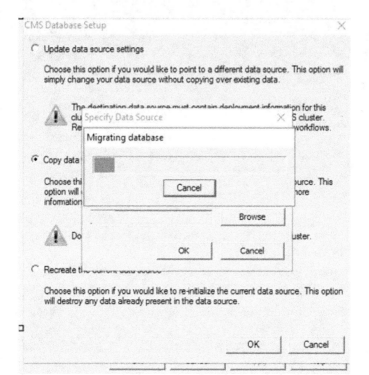

CMS Database Setup   ✕

  ◌ Update data source settings

     Choose this option if you would like to point to a different data source. This option will
     simply change your data source without copying over existing data.

    ⚠ The destination data source must contain deployment information for this
      clu Specify Data Source   ✕ S cluster.
      Re   workflows.
        Migrating database

  ◉ Copy data

     Choose thi   urce. This
     option will   Cancel   ore
     information

                  Browse

    ⚠ Do   uster.
            OK   Cancel

  ◌ Recreate the current data source

     Choose this option if you would like to re-initialize the current data source. This option
     will destroy any data already present in the data source.

                          OK   Cancel

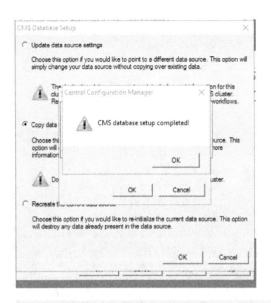

CMS Database Setup ×

C Update data source settings

Choose this option if you would like to point to a different data source. This option will
simply change your data source without copying over existing data.

⚠ The [...] on for this
clu Central Configuration Manager × S cluster.
Re workflows.

⚠ CMS database setup completed!

C Copy data

Choose thi [...] urce. This
option will [...] ore
information OK

⚠ Do uster.

OK Cancel

C Recreate t[...]

Choose this option if you would like to re-initialize the current data source. This option
will destroy any data already present in the data source.

OK Cancel

Properties | Dependency | Startup | Configuration | Protocol |

Server Intelligence Agent Command Line Options

Port Number:
6410

CMS System Database Configuration

Specify...

CMS belongs to cluster '

☐ Change Cluster Name to

CMS Cluster Key Configuration

Change...

OK Cancel Apply Help

141

Change the cluster key now, as it currently only contains the copied source system cluster key.

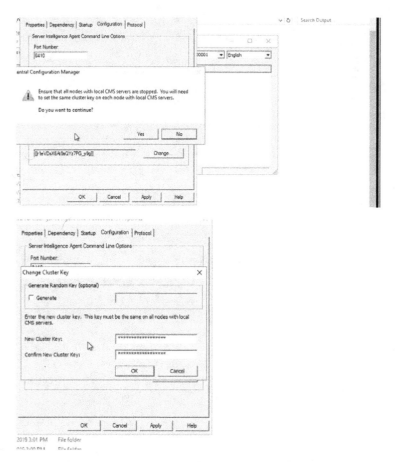

We need to recreate the node now, as this CMS currently contains all the servers in the node with copied system names.

Choose Recreate node option

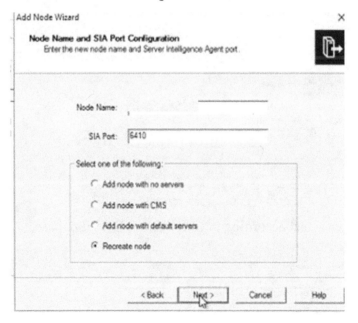

143

Choose 'start a new temporary CMS' option

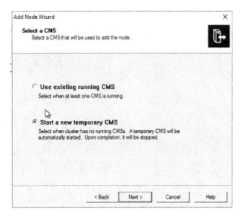

Please select according to your current CMS database.

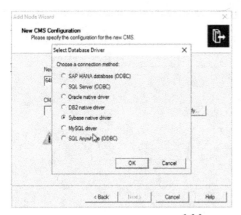

Provide the current CMS database details.

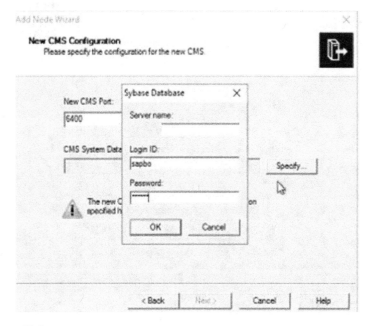

Click next

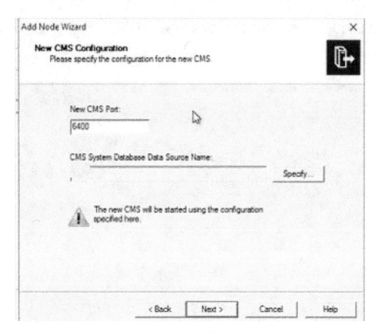

Click Next

Provide Cluster Key

Please provide the password for the older system administrator, as the CMS currently holds the credentials for the older system.

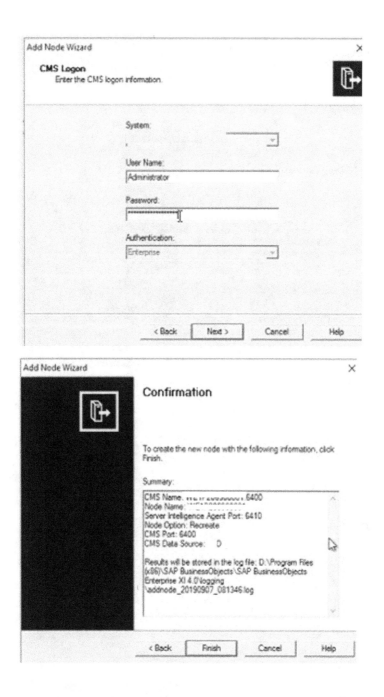

Adding node...

| | Cancel |

Central Configuration Manager

 Successfully added node.

View the log file for more details: D:\Program Files (x86)\SAP
BusinessObjects\SAP BusinessObjects Enterprise XI
4.0\logging\addnode_   log

| | OK |

SECTION 7 IMPLEMANTATION PLAN

Chapter 26 Implementation Plan

The implementation plan must include all necessary steps and timelines, organised into the following columns: 'Activity', 'Planned Start Date and Time (GMT)', 'Planned End Date and Time (GMT)', 'Number of Hours', 'Actual Start Date and Time (GMT)', 'Actual End Date and Time (GMT)', 'Number of Hours', and 'Status'. The list of activities is provided below.

Pre-implementation Checks

Check RAM, Processor & .net version, Space availability in server

Ports enabling between server and DB Server

Copy BO software in sever

Raise a request for empty DB creation on existing DB server and ask read, write and execute access privileges to - service account: XXXXXXX if service account is not existed raise a request with relevant team

DSN creation for Audit and CMS DB

Disable the Antivirus Status

Turn off DEP from Environment Variables

Drop an email to Application owner for approval to create SPN's and raise a request to relevant team to run and choose the right delegation

Implementation Checks

Logon to the server using service account

BI 4.2 installation and configuration

Configuration of BO services

Configuring CMC monitoring alerts (Watch List creation and configuration)

Windows AD Authentication & Configuration

Create SPN's and raise a request to Relevant team to run and choose the right delegation

Auditing Configuration

Single Sign on Configuration

DNS Configuration (Email to DNS Administrator Team)

Enable Antivirus Status and DEP